Fun with PAINT

Annalees Lim

WINDMILL BOOKS
New York

Published in 2013 by Windmill Books, An Imprint of Rosen Publishing
29 East 21st Street, New York, NY 10010

Copyright © 2013 by Wayland/Windmill Books, An Imprint of Rosen Publishing

Editor for Wayland: Victoria Brooker
US Editor: Sara Antill
Designer: Lisa Peacock
Photographer: Simon Pask
US Book Layout: Greg Tucker
Images used for creative graphics: Shutterstock
Cover picture: Thanks to Evelyn Burke

Library of Congress Cataloging-in-Publication Data

Lim, Annalees.
 Fun with paint / by Annalees Lim.
      p. cm. — (Clever crafts)
 Includes index.
 ISBN 978-1-4777-0182-9 (library binding) — ISBN 978-1-4777-0192-8 (pbk.) —
 ISBN 978-1-4777-0193-5 (6-pack)
 1. Handicraft—Juvenile literature. I. Title.
 TT160.L485 2013
 745.5—dc23

                          2012026227

Manufactured in the United States of America

CPSIA Compliance Information: Batch # BW13WM: For Further Information contact Windmill Books, New York, New York at 1-866-478-0556

Contents

Fun with Paint

You can have lots of fun with paint. In this book, you can paint with your fingers, with cotton swabs, and with scrunched up paper. You can even add different textures to the paint such as rice or oats.

You can also mix paints. Did you know that with just three colors, red, blue, and yellow, you can mix together a whole range of colors. These are called the three primary colors and by mixing them in different combinations, you can make any color you want!

Before you start painting, always cover surfaces with newspaper so it's easy to clear up any spills. Put on an apron or an old top. Find a space where you can leave your projects to dry. Then you're ready to paint!

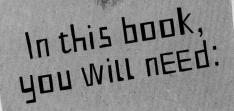

In this book, you will need:

Paint
Poster paints or acrylic paints are best for these projects.

Paintbrushes
It's good to have a few different-sized paintbrushes. Remember to always clean your paintbrush after you've finished your craft.

Colored cardboard or paper
To make your pictures and crafts with. You don't have to use the colors suggested in this book.

Glue
You can mix glue into your paint to make it stronger. Glue sticks are useful for sticking pictures to cardboard to make frames.

Scissors
Use child-size scissors. Ask an adult to help you with any tricky parts.

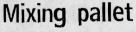

Mixing pallet
To hold the paint and to mix different colors

Color Wheel

You will need:

Thin cardboard
Compass
Pencil
Scissors
Ruler
Red, blue, and yellow paint
Paintbrush
Mixing pallet

You can have lots of fun with paint, but do you know what colors go well with others? Make this handy wheel to help you make great color choices and learn how to mix colors.

1

Draw a large circle on the cardboard with your compass. Cut out the circle.

2

Draw a line through the middle and then across to create 4 equal quarters. Divide each quarter into three to make twelve sections.

3

Paint a primary color (red, blue, and yellow) in each third of the circle, making sure there are three blank sections between each one.

4

Paint your secondary colors (purple, orange, and green) next. For purple, mix blue and red. For orange, mix red and yellow. For green, mix yellow and blue.

5

For the tertiary colors, mix whatever colors are either side of the blank section you want to fill. For example, mix primary yellow and secondary green to make light green.

Colors directly opposite each other on the color wheel are contrasting colors. This means they go well with each other. Colors that are beside each other on the color wheel are complimentary colors and work in harmony with each other.

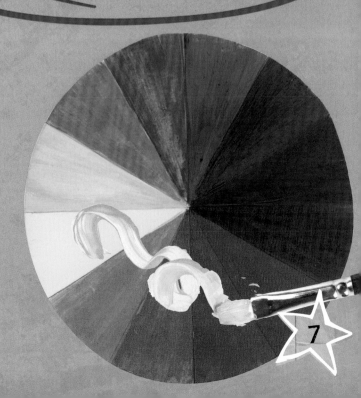

7

Handy Farmyard

Create a whole farmyard full of animals just by using your hands. First learn to print a whole herd of clucking chickens, and when you get the hang of it there are lots more animals you can try your hand at!

Fill your farmyard: Try printing a cow with horns and hoofs; a peacock with long feathers; a sitting duck with a beak and wings; or a sheep with a fluffy coat and tail.

You will need:
Paint
Paintbrush
White paper
Colored paper
Pen
Glue

1

Paint you whole hand any color you like.

2

Print your hand onto a white piece of paper and leave to dry.

3

Use a black pen to draw the outline of your chicken, using the handprint as a guide. Start drawing a head with a beak and wattle on the thumb.

4

Cut out your handprint chicken and glue it to a colored background. Try a green piece of paper to look like grass. Now try a different animal!

Wax Crayon Batik Owl

Batik was used by the ancient Egyptians. You can try it, too! This simple method uses just wax crayons and some watery paint.

You will need:
A pale colored crayon
White paper
Watered-down paint or watercolors
Cotton swab
Colored paper
Scissors
Glue

1

Draw a picture of an owl with your crayon. You could copy the one above or copy one from a book.

2

Mix some watery paints in your pallet. Paint over the whole page. Use different shades and blend them with water.

Use the same technique to send secret notes to friends. Write your note in crayon and ask your friend to paint over to reveal what you've said!

3

Before the paint completely dries use the cotton swab to wipe off the paint from the wax crayon lines. This will make the lines really bright.

4

Make a frame for your picture by folding a piece of construction paper in half and cutting out the middle. Make the sides uneven to make it look like the owl is poking out through leaves.

5

Glue the frame on top of your owl. Your owl picture is now ready to hang in your bedroom!

Bright Fireworks!

You will need:
Paint
Black paper or cardboard
Cotton swabs
Gray paper or cardboard
Scissors
Pencil
Ruler
Glue

Watch fireworks whizzing and banging in a starry sky all year-round by painting your own scene. You could make them really sparkle and shimmer by sprinkling the wet paint with glitter.

1

Paint a red firework in the middle of the black paper using a cotton swab to make the dots.

2

Paint two more fireworks in different colors either side using the same technique.

3

Paint bright yellow bursts of dots in the center of each firework and white dots on the outside. Leave to dry.

5

4

Glue the skyline onto the bottom of the black paper. Your picture is ready to display!

Draw a skyline onto the gray paper and cut it out.

Scrunched Seascape

You will need:
White paper
Paint
Scrunched-up newspaper
  or tissue paper
Scissors
Glue

Painting waves and sunny skies can take a while to learn, but with this simple technique you can create a fantastic seascape that will make you look like a master painter!

All sorts of shapes can be cut out of the painted paper to create different scenes.

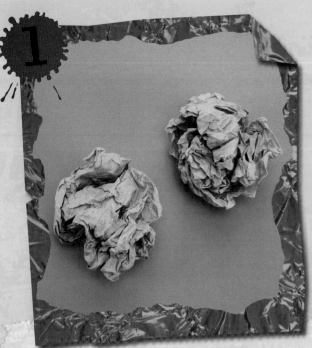

Scrunch up old pieces of newspaper or tissue paper into small balls.

Dunk the balls in paint and stamp them lightly all over a blank piece of paper. Make lots of sheets using different colors of paint.

Once the paper is dry, cut into shapes that will make your seascape. You will need some waves, a beach, a Sun, and a palm tree.

Stick your shapes onto a blue painted background. Try making different scenes using this technique.

Snowflake Wrapping Paper

Stencils are a quick and easy way to make repeat patterns and add a bit of color to any plain pieces of paper. The stencils are also really fun to make and, just like real snowflakes, they come out differently each time!

You will need:
Paper
Scissors
Paint
Paintbrush

1 Fold a piece of paper in half, then quarters, and then fold in half again to make a triangle shape.

2 Trim the top so it looks like an ice cream cone in shape.

3

Cut shapes into the cone shape. Open it up to reveal your snowflake stencil.

You could make the wrapping paper extra special by dabbing glue on and then sprinkling glitter on top.

4

Place the snowflake on a large piece of paper and dab paint through the holes of the stencil. Cover your whole piece of paper with snowflakes.

3-D Rainbow

You will need:
Mixing cups
Paint
Glue
Oats, rice, sugar, or pencil shavings
Compass
Pencil
Paper
Shiny or sparkly paper

Mix together this gloopy paint recipe to create a beautiful rainbow that really stands out from the page.

1

In a cup, mix 1 part glue to 3 parts paint. Add your chosen texture (oats, rice, sugar, or shavings) and mix well. Make four of these mixtures in different colors.

2

Using a compass, draw a semicircle to make the shape of a rainbow.

Try using the same technique to create waves in a seascape or to give to people fun hairstyles on top of faces you have painted.

3

Paint a thick line of textured paint onto the semicircle. Paint another line underneath and so on to create your rainbow.

4

Cut out shiny clouds and rain and glue these onto the picture to make your scene complete.

River Reflections

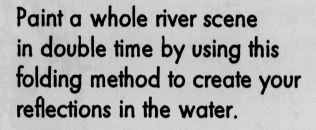

You will need:

Pale blue paper
Paintbrush
Paint

Paint a whole river scene in double time by using this folding method to create your reflections in the water.

1

Fold a piece of pale blue paper in half, long ways.

2

Paint the bottom half in a darker shade of blue. Use watery paint so that it looks more like a river.

You can print other reflections too. Try palm trees in a desert oasis or tall city buildings that are beside a wide river.

4

Fold the paper in half and press firmly. Open up carefully to reveal your river reflection!

3

Paint a landscape on the top half of the paper full of trees, bushes, and flowers.

Foil Prints

You will need:
Blank cards or folded plain paper
Tin foil
Scissors
Blunt pencil
Paint
Paintbrush

Tin foil that you find in your kitchen cupboards is not only useful when baking or cooking. It is a great craft material that you can use to make fantastic repeat patterns.

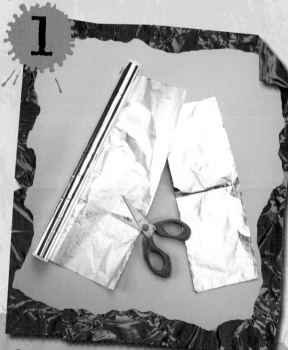

1

Cut a large piece of tin foil and fold it in half.

Try drawing the letters of your name to make a simple bedroom sign. Just remember to write everything backward so it prints the right way around!

2

Using a blunt pencil, draw an outline of a house. Press firmly so that it makes a deep dent. This is easier to do if you place the foil on a stack of magazines or papers.

3

Cover the drawing with a thin layer of paint.

4

Place the foil print on top of your blank card or folded paper and press firmly.

5

Carefully peel off the foil print. Your card print is ready to send. Try different pictures and colors.

Glossary

beak (BEEK) The hard part of a bird's mouth.

blunt (BLUHNT) Not sharp.

primary color (PRY-mer-ee KUH-ler) Red, yellow, and blue.

secondary color (SEH-kun-der-ee KUH-ler) A color made by mixing two of the primary colors together.

skyline (SKY-lyn) The outline of buildings against sky.

stencil (STEN-sul) Cutout patterns that can be used as guides for drawings or paintings.

technique (tek-NEEK) The particular way of doing something.

tertiary color (TER-shee-ayr-ee KUH-ler) A color made by mixing a primary and a secondary color together.

texture (TEKS-chur) The feel or look of a surface.

wattle (WAH-til) A flap of skin that hangs from the neck of a bird.

Index

Websites

For web resources related to the subject of this book, go to:
www.windmillbooks.com/weblinks
and select this book's title.